BEDTIME FOR NIGHTMARES

Written by
Matthew Bradley

Illustrations by
Augusto Zimiani

BEDTIME FOR NIGHTMARES

Written by
Matthew Bradley

Illustrations and Design by
Augusto Zimiani

On a day
Come what may
In my bed,
comfy,
I lay

When all
the worst voices in my head
started rustling
with something to say

I heard them coming

I heard whispers and wallows
until they became shouts

They were coming from all directions

So I wasn't sure if I was drifting within
or if they were drifting out

Together we met
They were all a fright
All the worst voices wanting control
All on the same night

The first voice came into my ears Like a soaking of honey in sticky bitter tears

...ul things that can make you happy and safe! In a cruel world of joyless pursuits, who doesn't deserve an escape? I can eat time that you might otherwise just waste! There is an indulgenc[e]... you had troubles! ALL I will ever ask is that you give me enough, if we're never satisfied with a feeling like this, that's what I call love."

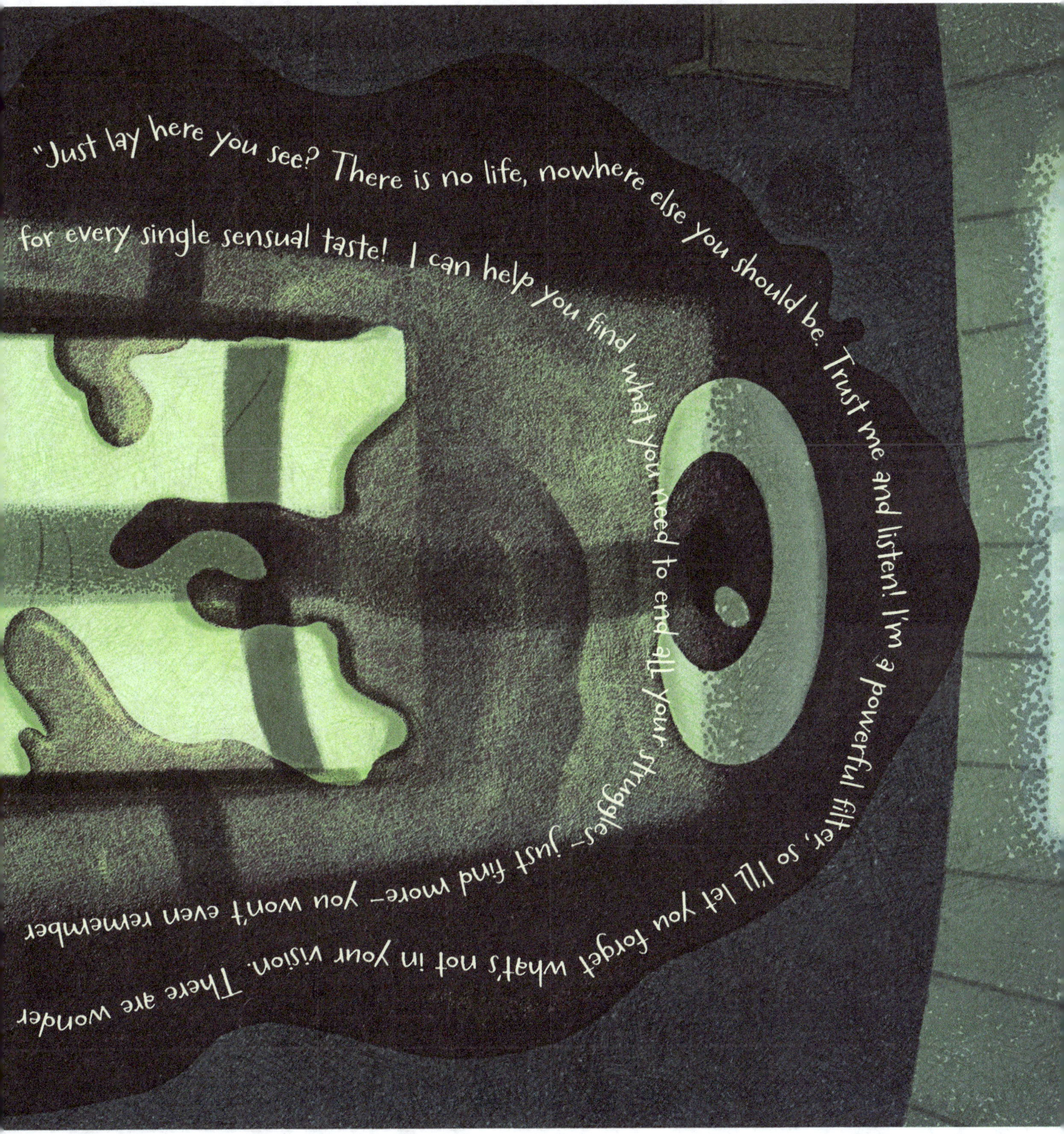

"Just lay here you see? There is no life, nowhere else you should be. Trust me and listen! I'm a powerful filter, so I'll let you forget what's not in your vision. There are wonder for every single sensual taste! I can help you find what you need to end all your struggles—Just find more—you won't even remember

But from the corner, came a voice malevolent with horror.
"Everyone is greater and nobody is great.
I secretly think the world is mine, but
I think about taking, and I think about
I would rather stay in, but you know outside
And if they reject us, it's because they're all
If we stay inside we may still step into the
them all feel alive or make them all

letting anyone know it would be a mistake.

keeping; I dream of revenge and other such tidings.

we must go; we have so much greatness that the world must know!

flawed. They're all weak and pathetic; they don't know I'm secretly a god.

Web. Through the power of words, we can make

wish they were dead."

Then came a meeker voice
from the corner

But this one spoke like a troll
and not like a spider

"Let's go find people! I'm hungry!
Other people's lives taste the best!
Self control for the sake of others is never a
success, and ending my own loneliness is
going to get intense! I'm really afraid but
I'll never admit it, control is the opposite
of chaos; insurance must always be heeded. I
am constantly in need, of very specific
desires. I can take all your worries and fears
and make anyone into a liar! I will name
myself with virtues but the truth is I'm just
conceited. You'll find that you follow in
whatever direction I lead in."

"Feed ME
Love ME
Respect ME!"

"If I can smell it, I want it. If I can taste it, I'll take it and if I can feel it, I've already swallowed it! Take all your negativity; I've got a cure! What can you drain from others that will taste the most pure? A giving heart is a resource; that you can be sure! I will show you the comforts without boundaries and life without regret! We may come off as callow, but we eat off the best! I won't ever be found alone in any way or sort, so I'll never be weak if I can feed off of a cohort. It's not quite abuse, and it's not quite love; I'll eat the bread of others and leave nothing but crumbs."

In a moment of broken mind
They had taken up all the space
And eaten up all the time
I lay there

There is nothing at all to wonder about. I want you to know
there's no reason to be alive, and all of your claims otherwise
are lies told by the mind. All existence is suffering, and you
are inferior. I live within you; I designed this interior. For
every choice you never made, whenever you were dismissive
of your emotional state, you were going ever deeper into
pain and self hate.

Trapped inside with them
Bearing thoughts
too horrible to mention

I have gained strength from every time you honored your mistakes. You are alone; my words become your reality when my words become your whole. I am the ego that is no more alive than dead; you've never been without me, as a pollution that you nurtured in the cosmos of your own head. ALL of you humans are nothing but a façade; it has been this way since you named your greatest fears "god."

What could I say now?
I was so very scared
But I didn't want to bow
If I had anything
to be called a soul
I knew it would be a mistake
to give any of them control
They were the names
for survival
and methods of class
Names as old as thought,
from the first to the last
Every human
unknowingly
bears such a torch
Keeping the world burning in a manner of sort

WHAT WAS I TO DO ???

It does no good to hate them

Make them small?
Try to KILL them all?
Change them with love?
Outlive them? Ignore them?
Join them? Bury them? Starve them?

They will not be silenced or banished.
You cannot just wait for the negative to vanish.

No.

The answer wasn't clear

I wanted to block out
what I didn't want to hear
Perhaps an answer
I might find in a mirror

Looking through my fears
made me forget
to listen
So it was then
I began speaking
through them

Here I stand
Accountable for my actions
I accept what I have done
And I may never truly be free

You're all the worst parts of my exhausted psyche
But your power declines when I can tell your voices from mine
I must have patience if I want to have time.
I need all of your voices to grow old, W i t h e r and die.

These monsters are everywhere, and
I'm not the only one seeing them

Some roam free, while others appear in phases
Everyone in their own minds travelling through personal mazes
We could be of more help to each other

If we could recognize the same struggle
on ALL human faces

Perhaps then, our free will could start taking us
to better places

BEDTIME FOR NIGHTMARES

Bedtime for Nightmares is dedicated to everyone who has taken the time and energy to understand then correct their own toxic traits. Humans are not always at fault for what has been done to them. No one asks for trauma; but for those who have been damaged and unwittingly pass on abuse, it is never easy to heal by way of changing behavior. Some go their whole lives without a second thought about the suffering going on around them, especially those who are themselves at fault. So this book is for those actively trying to make the world less toxic, starting with their own lives.

Matthew Bradley

This is Matthew Bradley's first publication. He would personally like to thank his Mother Debbie and his Daughter Chani for the inspiration and reason to explore the negative traits in his behavior. His forthright goals in life are to be a comic book writer and to continue urban farming.

Biorhythm is coming.

Follow on Instagram @matthewbradley238

Augusto Zimiani

This is also the first publication by Augusto Zimiani. He is a Brazilian illustrator who found in this project the chance to see his first book. He would like to thank his wife Stella and son Bernardo for their brilliant contributions, insights and inspiration. And also to thank Matthew for the trust with this wonderful project and for all the patience in dealing with the distance!

Follow on Instagram @zimiani